I love you
Dad...

I love you Dad...

and all the things you say and do

Susan Akass

illustrations by Hannah George

CICO BOOKS
LONDON NEW YORK

Published in 2011 by CICO Books
An imprint of Ryland Peters & Small
519 Broadway, 5th Floor,
New York NY 10012
20–21 Jockey's Fields,
London WC1R 4BW

www.cicobooks.com

10 9 8 7 6 5 4 3 2 1

Text © Susan Akass 2011
Design and illustration © CICO Books
2011

A CIP catalog record for this
bookis available from the Library
of Congress and the British Library.

ISBN: 978 1 907563 24 9

Printed in China

Design: David Fordham
Illustration: Hannah George

You have huge feet and I love wearing your shoes

You tickle me till I squeal

You have loads of cool gadgets

I love you,
because ....

You took me to a big game and our team won

We play great games with my diggers and cranes

You are brilliant at skimming stones

you act like a rock star and

Play air guitar

When you wash the car, you let me squirt the hose

squirt
squirt
squirt squirt

You tell scary stories with all the

actions

When you come to my room to switch off the light,

We secretly

play

COMPUTER GAMES

You watch
all my
soccer
matches,
even in the
rain

You have HUGE
feet and I love
wearing your
shoes.

We Went sledging together
and really

zoomED

You HATE putting together furniture, but you never give up

It was brilliant when we went to catch crabs (though I caught the BIGGEST one)

You like
fast cars and
we LOVE to spot
them together

You let
me ride
on your
shoulders

When I'm
too tired
to walk

When we went out in a boat, you let me steer

You know how to make stuff like bows and arrows, swords and shields, and paper aeroplanes

We flew
my kite
together
on a windy day

You helped me build

an **ENORMOUS**
SANDCASTLE
with moats and towers
and flags

You push me

higher and higher

on the swing

We both enjoy a challenge and you always get very

COMPETITIVE

When I
FALL
asleep in
the car,
you carry
me to bed

You help me with my sums and
claim it was different
when you
were at
school

We paddled together
in the sea and
JUMPED
Over the Waves

When you're driving the car you sing silly songs

You dressed up as
a VAMPIRE
and took us trick
or treating

We Play

GREAT

GAMES

with my

DIGGERS and CRANES

When I'm dressed
up for a party
you call me your
little princess

You took me to a
big game
and our team won

You're brilliant at skimming stones
skimming stones

When it's really
HOT you buy
me YUMMY
ice-cream to
COOL me down

When you are
in charge,
my clothes
NEVER
match

You
pretend
to be
a bear
and
chase
after
me

I've seen you sneak into the
kitchen and steal cookies

You tickle me till I squeal

When We Went to the
ZOO,
you made faces
at the monkeys

Your "best" sweater is full of HOLES but you refuse to

throw it away

When you cook,

you pretend you're a TV chef

You bought me a brand-new

BICYCLE

and taught me how to ride it